Welcome to
MYANMAR

Gareth Stevens Publishing
A WORLD ALMANAC EDUCATION GROUP COMPANY

Written by
DORA YIP/PAULINE KHNG

Designed by
LOO CHUAN MING

Picture research by
SUSAN JANE MANUEL

First published in North America in 2001 by
Gareth Stevens Publishing
A World Almanac Education Group Company
330 West Olive Street, Suite 100
Milwaukee, Wisconsin 53212 USA

For a free color catalog describing
Gareth Stevens' list of high-quality books
and multimedia programs, call
1-800-542-2595 (USA) or
1-800-461-9120 (CANADA).
Gareth Stevens Publishing's
Fax: (414) 332-3567.

© **TIMES EDITIONS PTE LTD 2001**
Originated and designed by
Times Editions
An imprint of Times Media Private Limited
A member of the Times Publishing Group
Times Centre, 1 New Industrial Road
Singapore 536196
http://www.timesone.com.sg/te

Library of Congress Cataloging-in-Publication Data
Yip, Dora.
Welcome to Myanmar / Dora Yip and Pauline Khng.
p. cm. -- (Welcome to my country)
Includes bibliographical references and index.
Summary: An overview of the geography, history, government,
economy, people, and culture of Burma, now known as Myanmar.
ISBN 0-8368-2520-9 (lib. bdg.)
1. Burma -- Juvenile literature. [1. Burma.]
I. Khng, Pauline. II. Title. III. Series.
DS527.4. Y59   2001
959.1--dc21   00-057350

Printed in Malaysia

1 2 3 4 5 6 7 8 9 05 04 03 02 01

PICTURE CREDITS
Archive Photos: 17
Bes Stock: 1, 20, 21 (top), 24, 34
Michele Burgess: 3 (center)
Ben Burt: 36 (top)
Focus Team — Italy: 22, 33
HBL Network Photo Agency: 21 (bottom)
Renata Holzbachová/Philippe Bénet: 29,
   32 (top), 37
Ingrid Horstmann: 18
Dave G. Houser: 10, 16, 19
The Hutchison Library: 26, 38
John R. Jones: 39
Richard I'Anson: cover, 25, 27,
   32 (bottom), 40
North Wind Picture Archives: 12
Christine Osborne Pictures: 41
Photobank Photolibrary: 36 (bottom), 43, 45
Pietro Scozzari: 2, 3 (bottom), 5, 28, 30, 31,
David Simson: 3 (top), 9 (both)
Tan Chung Lee: 7
Liba Taylor Photography: 23
Times Editions: 14, 35
Topham Picturepoint: 4, 8, 11, 13, 15 (top),
   15 (center)
Alison Wright: 6, 15 (bottom)

Digital Scanning by Superskill Graphics Pte Ltd

Contents

Words that appear in the glossary are printed in **boldface** type the first time they occur in the text.

Welcome to Myanmar!

Myanmar is a beautiful country with a rich history. It is a land of floating markets and golden pagodas. In 1989, the country's name was changed from *The Socialist Republic of the Union of Burma* to *The Union of Myanmar*. In this book, the old spelling of names is in parentheses. Let's visit Myanmar!

Opposite: Canals play an important role in the daily lives of villagers who live along them.

Below: Many people in Myanmar use wagons pulled by horses or oxen for transportation.

The Flag of Myanmar

The flag of Myanmar has a blue rectangle on a red background. In the rectangle are a cogwheel and a rice plant, which are surrounded by fourteen stars. The color blue symbolizes peace, and the color red represents courage.

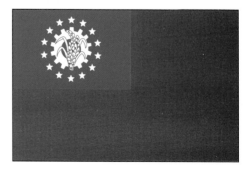

The Land

Shaped like a kite, Myanmar's landmass covers an area of 261,228 square miles (676,574 square kilometers). Myanmar is situated in Southeast Asia and is surrounded by five countries: India and Bangladesh to the west, China to the north, and Laos and Thailand to the east.

Myanmar's central plain has seen the rise and fall of many of its royal capitals. It receives little rainfall and is

Below: One of Myanmar's many temples is located on Mount Popa, the site of an extinct volcano.

also called the *dry zone*. About half of the country's population lives farther south on the Ayeyarwady (Irrawaddy) River **delta**. Although mountains cover half the country, few people live on the slopes.

The Thanlwin (Salween), Myanmar's longest river, flows into the Shan Plateau located in eastern Myanmar. It then empties into the Gulf of Mottama (Gulf of Martaban).

Climate

Myanmar has **monsoon** seasons. During the wet season, thunderstorms and heavy rain occur almost every day. During the dry season, temperatures are 70° Fahrenheit (21° Celsius) and above. The hottest months are March and April, when temperatures can be over 110° F (43° C). It is cooler in the mountains, and the northern mountain peaks can be snowcapped between November and January.

Above: Flooded rice fields often surround villages on the Shan Plateau.

Forests and Wildlife

Myanmar's natural vegetation is as varied as its climate. The southern parts are covered with tropical rain forests. Temperate oak and pine forests cover northern and high areas. **Mangrove** swamps often line the coast.

Myanmar is home to many animals, such as tigers, bears, and tapirs. Many birds nest in Myanmar. Poisonous snakes also live in this country.

Above: These lotus plants grow in wet areas all over Myanmar.

Left: The great hornbill is a rare bird species that makes its home in the forests of Myanmar.

History

The earliest people of Myanmar may have settled in the Ayeyarwady River area about 900 B.C. Between 100 B.C. and A.D. 800, an advanced people called the Pyu built great cities and temples in the north of the country. In the south, the Mon kingdom grew and

traded with India to its west. The Mon also spread their culture and their religion throughout Southeast Asia.

By the mid-ninth century, Chinese raids had weakened the Pyu. The Bamar (Burmans), a people the Pyu had ruled, came to power in the north.

Above: The Bamar built Bagan as their capital in about A.D. 849. Described today as a place of "exquisite ruins," it is located on the eastern bank of the Ayeyarwady River in central Myanmar.

Empires and Wars

In 1044, King Anawrahta was crowned. He made the north strong and conquered the Mon in the south. His **dynasty** lasted until 1247, when Mongols took the capital city, Bagan.

In 1531, King Tabinshwehti conquered the Mon and the Shan, who were fighting to control the country. He

started the Toungoo dynasty. The Mon rebelled and destroyed the capital in 1752, but a village headman named Aung Zeya formed an army to fight back. Aung Zeya became King Alaungpaya, "the Victorious," and started the Konbaung dynasty.

Above: As Western interests in Myanmar increased, the port of Yangon turned into an important trading center.

From British Rule to Independence

The British invaded Yangon in 1824 because Myanmar attacked British territories in India. Not until 1885, could the British reclaim the Indian territories and capture Myanmar's capital, Mandalay. Then the British ruled Myanmar as a part of India.

The British brought peace, but did not support the temples or the local economy. Many Burmese wanted independence. It took the British two years to **suppress** a 1930 rebellion.

Above: The British arrived in Mandalay in 1885 after fighting the Burmese for sixty years. They used elephants to carry their luggage.

In 1941, the Thirty Comrades, led by Burmese patriot Aung San, formed the Burma Independence Army (BIA). The BIA accepted Japanese control to get Japan's help in defeating the British. Although Japan made Burma independent in 1943, the Japanese still controlled Burma's leaders.

The BIA turned against Japan in 1945 and helped the British end Japan's rule in Burma. In meetings with the British, Aung San helped win Burma's independence. Sadly, he was **assassinated** six months before Myanmar's 1948 independence.

Left: The Japanese made full use of native labor as they advanced to Yangon (then called *Rangoon)* during World War II.

From Democracy to Military Rule

Following its first general election in 1951, Myanmar became a parliamentary democracy. However, unrest in villages and towns threatened the peace. In 1962, the army mounted a **coup d'etat** and set up a ruling Revolutionary Council.

Left: General Ne Win led the coup d'etat that took Myanmar down the road of military dictatorship. He was the chairman of the Burma Socialist Programme Party (BSPP) until 1988.

A wave of protests for democracy occurred during the 1980s. In 1988, General Saw Maung took over and brutally attacked supporters of democracy. Thousands of people died. Today, the struggle between military and democratic groups continues.

Aung San (1915–1947)

Aung San is widely regarded as the father of independent Myanmar. He fought hard for independence, first against the British, then against the Japanese. He was assassinated on July 19, 1947, six months before Myanmar was granted independence.

Aung San

U Nu (1907–1995)

U Nu became Myanmar's first prime minister in 1948. After the military gained power in 1962, U Nu was imprisoned. After his release in 1966, he fled to Thailand. He returned to Myanmar in 1980.

U Nu

Aung San Suu Kyi (1945–)

Aung San Suu Kyi, daughter of Aung San, helped form the National League for Democracy (NLD) in 1988. She was placed under house arrest from 1989 to 1995 because her popularity threatened the government. She was awarded the Nobel Peace Prize in 1991.

Aung San Suu Kyi

Government and the Economy

Myanmar is run by a military government. It is divided into seven divisions and seven states that consist of townships. The townships are made up of villages and wards.

The present head of state is General Than Shwe, who is the prime minister and chairman of Myanmar's ruling military group, the State Peace and Development Council.

Above: Yangon is the capital and largest city in Myanmar. It is also the country's political center. This picture shows City Hall.

The Armed Forces

Myanmar has the second largest armed forces in Southeast Asia. Known as the Tatmadaw, it has more than 429,000 members. Twenty-three military intelligence units work throughout the country to control any political **dissent**. A police force of about 50,000 helps enforce the harsh rules under which the people have to live. Under the military **regime**, thousands of innocent Burmese have been imprisoned.

Left: General Than Shwe inspects the Royal Guard-of-Honor at Parliament Square in Kuala Lumpur, Malaysia, in 1996.

A Struggling Economy

Myanmar's economy is one of the least developed in Southeast Asia. Most of its workers are involved in agriculture. Common crops include beans, corns, rice, sesame seeds, sugarcane, fruits, and vegetables.

Below: Agriculture plays a very important role in the economy of Myanmar.

The Black Market

When the military came to power, it took over the distribution of necessary household goods, such as rice and cooking oil. Demand for these goods was high, so shelves in government shops were often empty. As a result, a black market developed. People still trade illegally for certain items, including food and medicine.

Trade and Industry

Nine percent of Myanmar's workforce is employed in manufacturing industries.

The largest industry is processing fish and agricultural products. Textiles, mining, gas, and oil are also important.

Myanmar's main exports are rice, teak, minerals, and gems. Its trading partners include the European Union, Japan, China, India, and Singapore.

Above: Busy ports, such as Yangon's port on the Hlaing (Rangoon) River, are ideal places for vendors to sell their goods.

People and Lifestyle

There are officially 135 minority groups in Myanmar. Most of these groups live in the hills, and they each have their own lifestyle and language. Over the years, they have tried to preserve their own individual cultures.

About 70 percent of the people in Myanmar are descendants of the Bamar, who came from Central Asia and Tibet more than twelve hundred years ago. The Shan make up 8.5 percent of the population and the Kayin make up 6.2 percent.

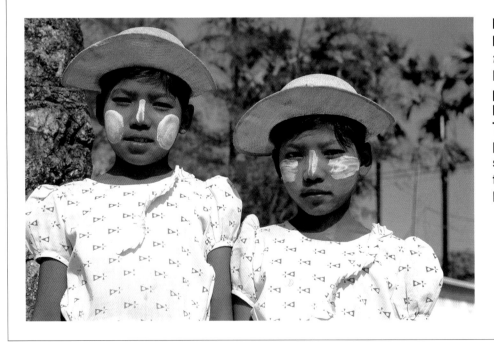

Left: Many Burmese put *thanaka* (th'-nah-KAH), a yellowish paste made from bark, on their faces. They believe the paste prevents sunburn and stops the skin from becoming oily.

Left: These men are from the Taungyo minority that lives in Shan state.

Etiquette is very important to the Burmese. It is not proper to show too much emotion in public. Elders should be treated with courtesy. On formal occasions, the Burmese show their respect by kneeling down and touching the ground with their foreheads and elbows. Whenever they pass a pagoda or meet a monk, they put their palms together as a sign of respect.

The Burmese are also sensitive about inconveniencing others. This fear of embarrassing others is called *anade* (AH-nar-DEH).

Below: Women of the Padaung ethnic minority are famous for their neck rings. These neck rings can weigh up to 20 pounds (9 kilograms)!

Family Life

Family is very important to the Burmese. Three generations often live under the same roof. Children learn to share from a young age. Siblings and cousins often share bedrooms. Children also learn to respect and obey their parents and elders at an early age.

Above: If family members do not live in the same house, they visit each other often.

Women in Burmese Society

Buddhists in Myanmar believe that men have a higher status than women, and that the husband is the spiritual head of the household. Nevertheless, women are fairly independent. They run the home and often have a small business, too. Many women sell food or trade goods in markets. Other women have professional jobs in medicine, law, dentistry, or education. In Myanmar, an equal number of men and women enroll at universities.

Below: Many Burmese women walk to market, often balancing their goods in large baskets on their heads.

Education

In Myanmar, school is required from ages 5 to 9. From kindergarten to Standard 2, at about age 8, children learn Burmese, English, and arithmetic. At Standards 3 and 4, they add geography and history. About 75 percent of Myanmar's students drop out after Standard 4, at about age 10, to work with their families.

Students who do not drop out work very hard in school. A diploma or degree will help them get good jobs.

Below: Schoolchildren in Mandalay work very hard so that they do well at school. A normal school day begins at 9 a.m. and ends at 3 p.m. Some schools have so many students that they split the day into two sessions.

Studying for university placement tests is also important because only one in five students who applies to a university is accepted. The oldest universities in Myanmar are the Universities of Yangon and Mandalay.

Above: These schoolchildren in Yangon enjoy going to school.

The military government has closed Myanmar's universities since 1996, but students from well-off families attend universities in other countries, such as the United States, the United Kingdom, and Australia.

Religion

Almost 90 percent of Myanmar's people are Buddhists. Buddhists believe in doing good deeds and attaining **enlightenment**. They try to live according to the Five Precepts,

Below: A procession of Buddhist nuns makes its way to a temple.

which state that Buddhists must not lie, steal, kill, take intoxicants (such as alcohol), or commit sexual misconduct.

Other religions in Myanmar include Christianity and Islam. Western missionaries brought Christianity to Myanmar hundreds of years ago.

Myanmar's Muslim population lives mainly in Rakhine state. The hill minorities also worship different kinds of spirits that vary from group to group. Those spirits are different from the ***nat*** (NAHT) spirits, or wandering souls, that are worshiped by some Burmese.

Language

The Burmese language is based on different tones. Words that are spelled the same can have very different meanings if the words are said with a higher or lower sound.

Modern Burmese has developed over the years. Today, the Burmese language has thirty-two consonants and twelve vowels.

The spoken form of the language is called **colloquial** Burmese. Literary Burmese — the written form — is used in official documents, newspapers, and textbooks. It differs from colloquial Burmese in a few aspects of grammar and vocabulary.

Above: The Burmese script comes from the ancient Pali language of India and Ceylon (now Sri Lanka).

Literature

The people of Myanmar love to read. However, books are scarce because the country is poor. Myanmar has only about three hundred public libraries. All locally produced works are carefully reviewed by the government. Many writers and cartoonists have been jailed for their political statements against the military regime.

The most famous Burmese writer is Ma Ma Lay. Her novel *Not Out of Hate* was the first Burmese book to be published in English.

Below: The Burmese can rent out books and magazines from *sa-ok-hnga-hsaing* (sar-oak-HNGA-sayng), or book rental shops.

Arts

Myanmar is a land of rich artistic tradition. Its pagodas are adorned with beautiful **friezes** and wall paintings. Myanmar's minority hill tribes also have their own arts and crafts.

Marionette Theater

Marionette performances are based on stories about the Buddha's past lives. The puppets have up to eighteen strings

Below: Puppeteers, singers, and an orchestra make up a puppet troupe.

and are about 22-27 inches (59-69 cm) tall. They were very popular in the nineteenth century. Today, however, their popularity has been overtaken by videos and movies.

Kalaga

Kalaga (kah-lah-gah), or richly embroidered cloth, was used by monks, royalty, and rich people as portable curtains. The lengths of cloth could be hung with rope from trees, posts, or pillars to create private areas.

Gold Leaf

Gold leaf is used to coat items such as musical instruments and religious images. Lumps of gold are flattened by a machine, and then hand-beaten until they are as thin as a layer of paint. The gold sheets are cut into small squares and sold in bundles that measure about 2 inches (5 cm). Mandalay is the center of the gold leaf industry in Myanmar.

Above: Myanmar is famous for its pagodas. Kyaiktiyo Pagoda, or the Golden Rock, is an important shrine for pilgrims. It is 80 feet (24.4 meters) high!

Left: Many Buddhist worshipers buy thin squares of gold leaf to stick onto the Golden Rock.

Left: Unlike the Western-style harp, the Burmese harp is rested on the harpist's lap. It is shaped like a boat and has sixteen strings.

Music

Traditional Burmese music uses many kinds of drums. In fact, drum names are used to describe different types of music, songs, and dances.

Traditional Burmese orchestras include a drum section with nine to twenty-one drums. Gongs, flutes, and other clappers and cymbals are placed in a circle around a single performer. Western instruments can also be added.

Leisure

Most people enjoy free outdoor events, such as festivals and *pwe* (PWAIR), a mix of music, drama, and dance.

Many of these performances last throughout the night, and might even go on for a few days! In the countryside, people roll out their grass mats, sit back, and enjoy the show.

The people of Myanmar enjoy watching movies. Myanmar imports most of its movies, although locally

Below: The Burmese often wait in very long lines to see their favorite movies.

34

made movies do exist. Most of the Burmese films revolve around love stories and often include lots of singing and dancing.

Children's Games

Burmese children are good at turning old household items into toys. They make slingshots from twigs and rubber bands and fold bits of paper into boats, birds, and boxes. They also enjoy playing group games.

Above: Burmese children spend hours playing games that use their fingers or hands. *Kyet-pyan-nghet-pyan* (CHET-pyahn-NGHET-pyahn), or "Hens Fly, Birds Fly," is one popular game. Children sit in a circle and take turns to name an object. If they name a flying animal or object, the other players have to raise their hands. If a player makes a mistake, he or she is out of the game.

Sports

Boxing and rowing are popular sports in Myanmar. Traditional boat races often take place during festivals that are held during the rainy season.

Chinlon (CHIN-LONE), a game played with a rattan ball, is exciting to watch — players have to keep the ball in the air without using their hands.

Forms of self defense, such as judo and *thaing* (THINE), a Burmese martial art, are popular throughout Myanmar.

Above: Boat races held on Inle Lake are unique. Participants wrap one leg around an oar and move the boat through the water, standing up.
Below: Players of all ages enjoy playing chinlon.

Cockfights are widespread in the countryside and often draw large crowds of supporters. Spectators place bets on the bird they think will win.

People in the cities enjoy tennis, golf, soccer, basketball, and other common sports.

Festivals

The people of Myanmar love festivals. Some festivals involve celebrations throughout the country; others are celebrated locally.

Thingyan, or the Water Festival, begins in the Burmese New Year. The festival lasts three to five days. During the festivities, people splash water on passersby, friends, and relatives to wash away bad luck. On New Year's Day, people release captive fish and birds and hold special feasts for monks.

Above: Just about everyone is soaked during Thingyan, the Water Festival.

The Buddhist Lent lasts for three months. It begins with the Waso Robe Offering Ceremony in June or July and ends with the Festival of Lights, which is held in September or October. During the Festival of Lights, Myanmar becomes a world of blazing lanterns, candles, and electric lightbulbs.

The Weaving Festival is celebrated in October and November. At all-night weaving contests in the pagodas, people make robes for Buddha images.

Below: Shin-byu **novitiates** form part of the New Year's Day parades in Bagan.

Food

Burmese food has Indian and Chinese influences. Cooks use a variety of spices and cooking styles to bring out the flavor of the food. Fish sauce and fish paste are also commonly used.

Lepet is a **condiment** that is unique to Myanmar. It is made from pickled tea leaves soaked in oil and crushed garlic.

Fruits and vegetables are plentiful in Myanmar. The jackfruit is a huge fruit that can weigh up to 80 pounds (36 kg)! Its yellow flesh is sweet, and

Left: Streetside food stalls throughout Myanmar sell a variety of tasty vegetable and meat fritters.

its seeds can be eaten like nuts. An unusual fruit is the durian, which is known for its very strong odor. Other common fruits include pineapples, mangoes, papayas, rambutans, mangosteens, and pomelos.

Eating in Myanmar

Burmese dishes are placed on the table all at once and are eaten at the same time. Most people eat with their fingers, sitting around low, round tables.

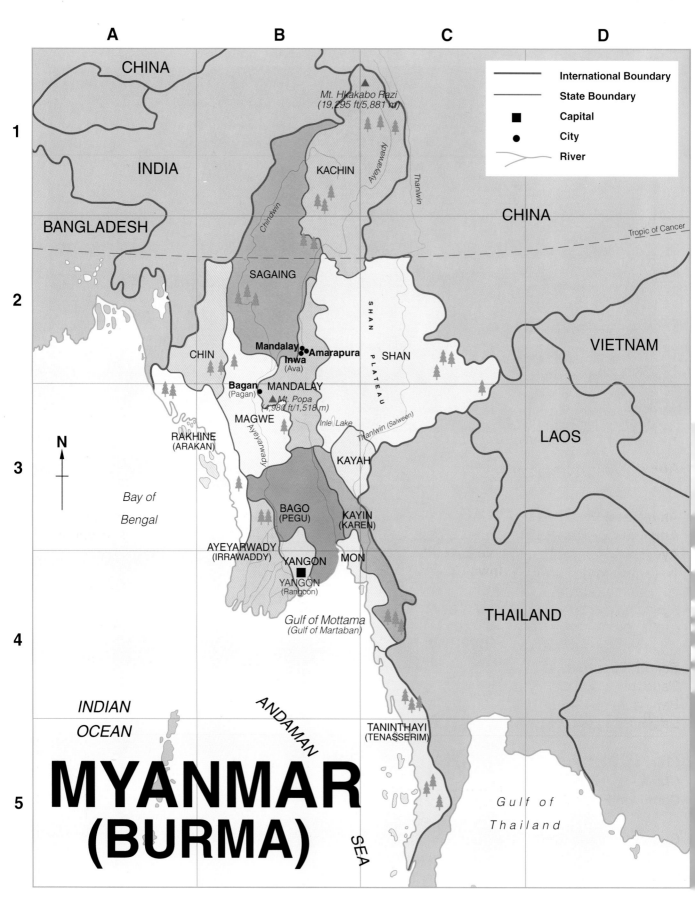

MYANMAR (BURMA)

Above: Women working in the rice fields of Amarapura.

Amarapura B2
Andaman Sea B4–B5
Ayeyarwady
(Irrawaddy),
division B3–B4
Ayeyarwady River
C1–B4

Bagan (Pagan) B3
Bago, division B3–B4
Bangladesh A1–A2
Bay of Bengal A3

Chin, state A2–B2
China A1, C1–D2
Chindwin River B1–B2

Gulf of Mottama (Gulf
of Martaban) B4
Gulf of Thailand C5–D5

India A1–B1
Indian Ocean A4–A5
Inle Lake B3
Inwa (Ava) B2

Kachin, state B1–C1
Kayah, state B3–C3
Kayin (Karen), state
B3–C4

Laos C3–D3

Magwe, division
B2–B3
Mandalay, city B2
Mandalay, division
B2–B3
Mon, state B3–C4
Mount Hkakabo
Razi C1
Mount Popa B3

Rakhine (Arakan),
state A3–B3

Sagaing, division
B1–B2
Shan, state B2–C3
Shan Plateau C2–C3

Taninthayi
(Tenasserim),
division C4–C5

Thailand C3–D5
Thanlwin (Salween)
River C1–B3

Vietnam D2–D3

Yangon (Rangoon),
city B4
Yangon, division
B3–B4

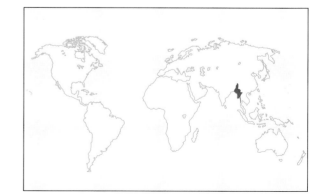

Quick Facts

Official Name   The Union of Myanmar

Capital   Yangon (Rangoon)

Official Language   Burmese

Population   48,081,302 (July 1999 estimate)

Land Area   261,228 square miles (676,574 square km)

States   Chin, Kachin, Kayah, Kayin, Mon, Rakhine, Shan

Divisions   Ayeyarwady, Bago, Magwe, Mandalay, Sagaing, Taninthayi, Yangon

Highest Point   Mount Hkakabo Razi at 19,295 feet (5,881 m)

Major Rivers   Ayeyarwady, Chindwin, Thanlwin (Salween)

Main Religion   Theravada Buddhism (89 percent)

Major Festivals   Buddha Day (Banyan Tree Watering Festival)

Burmese New Year

Festival of Lights

Harvest Festival

The Weaving Festival

Thingyan (Water) Festival

Waso Robe Offering Ceremony

Currency   Kyat (K 6.25 = U.S. $1 in 2000)

Opposite: The Royal Palace is in Mandalay.

44

Glossary

anade (AH-nar-DEH): in Burmese etiquette, the practice of showing consideration for others by not embarrassing them.

assassinated: killed for political reasons.

chinlon (CHIN-LONE): a Southeast Asian game played with a cane ball. Players keep the ball in the air using any part of the body except the hands.

colloquial: describing everyday or informal speech or writing.

condiment: a substance added to food to increase the flavor.

coup d'etat: a political uprising resulting in a change of government.

delta: a flat plain that forms from the material deposited by a river when it reaches the sea.

dissent: strong disagreement.

dynasty: a family inheriting power.

enlightenment: the state of intellectual or spiritual understanding.

etiquette: a set of customs and rules for polite behavior.

friezes: decorative carved panels, usually at the tops of walls.

kalaga (kah-lah-gah): a richly embroidered piece of cloth traditionally used for curtains.

kyet-pyan-nghet-pyan (CHET-pyahn-NGHET-pyahn): "Hens Fly, Birds Fly," a children's game in which players name an object and raise their hands only for flying objects.

mangrove: a seaside tropical tree with interlacing roots above the ground.

marionette: a puppet controlled by strings.

monsoon: a season of heavy rain.

nat (NAHT): in traditional Burmese beliefs, the spirits of people who have suffered violent or tragic deaths.

novitiates: people admitted into a religious order for a trial period before they take vows.

pwe (PWAIR): a traditional form of entertainment or performance.

regime: a system of government; a government currently in power.

sa-ok-hnga-hsaing (sar-oak-HNGA-sayng): book rental shops in Myanmar.

suppress: to use force to stop something from continuing.

thaing (THINE): a Burmese martial art and form of self defense.

thanaka (th'-nah-KAH): a light yellow paste made of bark.

More Books to Read

Aung San Suu Kyi: Fearless Voice of Burma. Newsmakers Biographies series. Whitney Stewart (Lerner)

Aung San Suu Kyi: Standing Up for Democracy in Burma. Women Changing the World series. Bettina Ling and Charlotte Bunch (Feminist Press)

Burma. Cultures of the World series. Saw Myat Yin (Benchmark Books)

Burma. Enchantment of the World series. David K. Wright (Children's Press)

Burma: Encountering the Land of the Buddhas. Ellis Everarda (Weatherhill)

Burmese Dance and Theatre. Images of Asia series. Noel F. Singer (Oxford University Press)

Celebrate in Southeast Asia. Joe Viesti (William Morrow and Co. Library)

In the Forest with the Elephants. Roland Smith and Michael J. Schmidt (Gulliver Books)

The Wise Washerman: *A Folktale from Burma.* Deborah Froese (Hyperion Books for Children)

Videos

Mission of Burma: Live at the Bradford. (Video Music Distribution)

Mystic Lands — Burma: Triumph of the Spirit / Jerusalem: Mosaic of Faith. (Fox / Lorber)

Web Sites

www.link.lanic.utexas.edu/asnic/ countries/myanmar

www.holidayfestival.com/Burma.html

www.myanmar.com

myanmars.net/arts/

Due to the dynamic nature of the Internet, some web sites stay current longer than others. To find additional web sites, use a reliable search engine with one or more of the following keywords to help you locate information about Myanmar. Keywords: *Aung San, Aung San Suu Kyi, Burmese, pagodas, Thingyan festival, Yangon.*

Index